Day Moon Fading

Also by Judith E.P. Johnson

Mountain Moods (VDL Publications, 1997)

Gatherers (VDL Publications, 1998)

Fragments (VDL Publications, 2000)

Selected Poems CD (7 RPH, 2001)

Snapshot (Regal Press, 2003)

Landmarks (Ginninderra Press, 2005)

Alone at the Window (Ginninderra Press, 2012)

Between Two Moons (Ginninderra Press, 2015)

Waking from Dreams (Ginninderra Press, 2016)

Where It Leads (Ginninderra Press, 2018)

Only the Waves (Ginninderra Press, 2019)

Briefly in Spring (Ginninderra Press, 2020)

Judith E.P. Johnson

Day Moon Fading

haiku & senryu

Acknowledgements

The author has had many haiku presented in journals, on radio, and online. The haiku in *Day Moon Fading* are new and unpublished, except for those which appeared in *Echidna Tracks*, *Windfall* and *Ko*.

Special thanks are due to Peter Macrow for his kindness and inspiration, to my children Karen, Debra, and Craig, for their encouragement and support, to Jane Williams for editing this book, and to Katherine Johnson for the cover design.

Day Moon Fading: haiku & senryu
ISBN 978 1 76109 205 3
Copyright © text Judith E.P. Johnson 2021
Cover: Katherine Johnson

First published 2021 by
GINNINDERRA PRESS
PO Box 3461 Port Adelaide SA 5015
www.ginninderrapress.com.au

for Graeme

Foreword
By Toshio Kimura

The poet's gaze on nature –

Each haiku is not a mere poetic sketch, but a journey to explore the mysteries hidden behind. In *Day Moon Fading*, Judith E.P. Johnson suggests the secrets in familiar matters.

> river reflections
> day moon ghosting
> not there

The midday moon, not lying on the surface, is watching over the poet from the sky throughout the collection.

> shutting my book
> hidden shadows
> escape

> around us
> gathering shadows
> of those not there

These are about things which you do not notice when you are deep in work, but surely you are not alone....

>   flying high
>   two doves
>   on the willow pattern plate

Doves are flying in the sky... However, they themselves might have been paintings in the patterns of the plate – now released from it.

>   beach campfire
>   the blue flame
>   of driftwood

We have seen the flame of the campfire – when we read this haiku, we can imagine where the sharp blue colour of it came from.

>   falling
>   even all these blossom
>   return to dust

We realise that not only the blossoms but we, though not depicted here, are heading for where we used to be.

> fragile
> this old Book of Dreams
> long forgotten

> reading alone
> the ache
> of poetry

Here, readers imagine the pleasure and pain of reading. *Day Moon Fading* is a fantastic haiku collection.

Toshio Kimura
Professor of English, Nihon University, Tokyo, and author of the haiku collections *In the Distance* and *Little Brier-Rose*

clear sky
high above dolphins
day moon fading

bushwalk
the child stops to hug
a sapling

wilderness
she carries out
a lyrebird's feather

garden fence
freesias scent the air
unseen

dead hibiscus
only a bee saw it
in full bloom

beach park
mown grass underfoot
the midden

planting a tree
she loosens its roots
into earth worms

rippling
over pebbles
moon shadows deepen

ups and downs
playing with grandchildren
snakes and ladders

leafy twitter
a sudden silence
as I pass

heatwave
even in moonlight
the heat

lavender farm
sunlit haze alive
with bees

summer
running through my fingers
the sand

beach campfire
the blue flame
of driftwood

vertical shoebox
the long-eared bat
recovering

passing the hedge
a shock of pain
death of a bee

sun's last rays
a butterfly
closes its wings

birthday wish
cutting the cake
only I know

midnight sky
a red flower
explodes overhead

open doorway
black cat
joins the moon

forty years on
kimono just right
now too long

out of sight
still in my mind
wild anemone

bedtime
I settle my bones
into dreams

first love
in her whispered name
young again

my childhood death wish
to die
before the dog

noisy welcome
at my daughter's house
new puppy

fragile
this old Book of Dreams
long forgotten

up early
after the nightmare
a cup of tea

winter solstice
a weak sun
blurs the moon

cold on my palm
green frog's
little hands

for a while
we walk together
winter sun

after the lights
of Dark Mofo
Aurora Australis

running water
the bright-eyed trout
fishmonger's window

tiny eggs
on a gnarled tree trunk
mottled sunlight

sky-deep river
a black swan drifts
on clouds

around us
gathering shadows
of those not there

waterfall
through tree ferns
the misty rainbow

shutting my book
hidden shadows
escape

door bell
I put a bookmark
in the haunted castle

star-crossed day
at last
the rising moon

sunrise
the night sky disappears
behind the mountain

from a dream forgotten
I awake
to tears

lakeside hotel
a pansy decorates
the grilled trout

carved bust from Bali
birds and flowers
in her hair

spring showers
around the child
so many blossoms to come

fish shadow
green frog leaps
lily pad to lily pad

falling
even all these blossom
return to dust

baby and dog
for each her voice
the same

gusty dog beach
a puppy grabs
the end of my scarf

midnight moon
somewhere the tide
is sifting shells

marine life
deep beneath a cruise ship
mountains and valleys

rock-a-bye, rock-a-bye
waking up
in the storm

swaying deck
one step forward
two steps back

returning
after twelve days at sea
the stillness

approaching landfall
a pleasure boat disappears
into the long white cloud

tropical fish and coral
marine tank
behind the hotel desk

spring cleaning
in my cupboards
the too hard basket

sewing box secret
in a compartment
the mariner shell necklace

morning traffic
has anyone noticed
the lingering moon

youthful exploit
each time he tells it
more daring

childhood recall
true or not
it is so

heavy rain
I walk for half an hour
on the treadmill

sunshine
the water jug
fills with light

sympathy card
in print
words he couldn't say

without saying sorry
he buys her
an ice cream

a line of ants
up the wall
one turns back

thinking of something
she turns back
wanting to stay

windswept clouds
now you see it, now you don't
the midday moon

garden coffee
trembling under my chair
the pink oxalis

breakfast sunshine
the dog's tail thumps
the biscuit cupboard

spring flowers
on a family plot
the blank plaque

artificial butterflies
touching one
it takes flight

calm day
leaves fall
of their own accord

poplar leaves falling
I look up
and up

picking violets
mother's childhood
memories

window chair
she knits the day
into a scarf

river reflections
day moon ghosting
not there

sunrise
motionless I stand
earth turning

holding my breath
a butterfly
on my finger

blossom sky
small child
in the old pear tree

so far below
cracked ice
on mountain lakes

on the phone
nodding in agreement
budding leaves

a secret once told
anyone's secret
gusty winds

emptying the car
filling the shack
long weekend

sibling get-together
shared memories
differ

apart
yet you are still with me
full moon

delicate
in bush debris
skeleton leaf

dearly beloved…
a blackberry vine
covers the name

deep within me
an old happiness
still glowing

packed theatre
I lose myself
in the music

going through the motions
my thoughts elsewhere
morning mist

reading alone
the ache
of poetry

shadows lengthen
we sit over
another cup of tea

flying high
two doves
on the willow pattern plate

time to go
we stand talking
on the doorstep

stay
don't go yet
full moon rising

www.ingramcontent.com/pod-product-compliance
Lightning Source LLC
Chambersburg PA
CBHW062201100526
44589CB00014B/1894